Hymns About Jesus

by Thomas Tiplady

Printed for the author
by
THE EPWORTH PRESS
LONDON

O Men of God, go forth to win
    The world for Jesus Christ your Lord;
With faith that glows, and love that burns,
    Proclaim to all His gracious Word.

To North and South, to East and West,
    Go forth in Christ's most holy Name;
On every hill a beacon light,
    And set the world with truth aflame.

Let nothing daunt your ardour pure,
    Nor turn you from your purpose great;
To save a world Christ sends you out,
    And for your message millions wait.

On Calvary the Saviour died
    For every man of every race;
'Tis yours to make the good news known,
    And be the channels of His grace.

Hymns About Jesus

I

The Annunciation

St Luke 1 : 26-35

6.5.6.5.

1 In the happy Springtime
   An Archangel came
To the lowly maiden
   That we Mary name.

2 Happy was the maiden
   In that Springtime fair;
For the news he brought her
   Was beyond compare!

3 In the dark mid-winter,
   When the rose had fled,
There would come her Saviour
   By sweet angels led;

4 In her arms to nestle—
   Word of God made flesh—
Fairer than the moonlight
   In its cloudy mesh;

5 In her arms to nestle,
   Such a small, sweet thing!
He who made the starlight
   She to sleep would sing!

6 Glory, laud and honour
   Be to God on high,
Who, to our redeeming,
   Brought a mother's cry.

The First Christmas Day

Brahms's Slumber Song. 6.6.6.6.6.6.6.6.

1   Over Bethlehem's town,
    Where the winter was mild,
There was heard a sweet song
    At the birth of a Child :
It was long, long ago
    When the world was still new;
And the Babe was as fair
    As a rose wet with dew.

2   Shepherds came from their folds
    To keep watch by the bed
Of the Lamb that was born
    In the cold cattle shed :
And these men from the hills,
    Who were keepers of sheep,
Softest wool did present
    For the Baby's first sleep.

3   There was glory on high,
    And on earth there was peace;
For the song angels sang
    Was of love's rich increase;
And when Mary her Babe
    In the manger did lay,
All the hopes of the world
    Lay asleep on the hay.

A Hymn of the Nativity

8.8.8.7 with Chorus

Blow, winds, O softly blow;
Bring flowers instead of snow;
Let blossoms deck the trees
    A Babe to please.

1   The winter morn comes gently down
    The quiet streets of David's town,
    And, in a manger old and brown,
        A little Child is sleeping.

            Blow, winds, etc.

2   Sing, angels, sing a lullaby
    Or He too soon may learn to cry :
    Yea, sing the songs He knew on high,
        Lest He for heav'n be grieving.

            Blow, winds, etc.

3   Draw near, O shepherds, to His bed,
    For lambs ye oft have nursed and fed;
    And 'tis God's Lamb that lays His head
        Within this humble manger.

            Blow, winds, etc.

4   O Wise Men, hasten on your way
    With gifts for Him to toy and play;
    For He who made your star's bright ray
        Is lying in this manger.

            Now men of every race
            Joy light the way you trace.
            And lead you bravely on
            To Mary's Son.

5

When Christmas Bells began to Chime

8.8.8 8 8 8.

1 Lord Jesus, in the winter time,
    And to a world grown old in sin,
Thou in Thy loveliness didst come,
    And as a child didst enter in;
The world was glad for Thee, and rang
    With carols herald angels sang.

2 Thy birth, it was the springtime sweet,
    The harbinger of summer time;
The sad, old world renewed its youth
    When Christmas bells began to chime;
And faith and hope, love, peace and mirth,
    Sprang up, like flowers, o'er all the earth.

3 And now, Lord, to this heart of mine,
    So wintry, sad, and soiled with sin,
Come, as Thou cam'st to Bethlehem,
    And let it be Thy wayside inn;
O come, then winter shall depart
    And springtime blossom in my heart.

III

The Boyhood of Jesus
St Luke 2 : 39-52

St Denis. 11.11.11.11.

1 Away in a cottage in old Galilee,
   A Boy, with His mother, lives blithesome and free;
The birds sing their sweetest when walking goes He,
   And spring hangs her blossoms on every green tree.

2 The cattle, though grazing, look up when they hear
   The footsteps of Jesus, and nothing they fear;
The sheep with their lambkins, where sweet waters glide,
   Come running to meet Him and walk by His side.

3 Old people grow wistful, and after Him look
   As, passing their cottage, He fords the clear brook :
They think of a story by shepherds once told,
   And dream of the kingdom that prophets behold.

IV

The Divine Workman

All things were made by Him; and without Him was not anything made that was made. And the Word was made flesh and dwelt among us.

St. John 1 : 3, 14

11.11.11.11.

1 Away in a village in sweet Galilee
  Where time ripples onward like streams to the sea,
A young Man is making a plough from a tree
  That golden, with harvest, the fields may soon be.

2 The shavings fall softly and curled at His feet,
  They fill the plain workshop with fragrance most sweet :
He sings, as He labours, a song, soft and low,
  To music the shepherds of Bethlehem know.

3 The merchantmen's camels pass slowly His door,
  And Rome's hardy legions march by as of yore;
But, heedless, this Workman works on as before,
  For He shall be worshipped when Rome is no more.

4 He comforts young children by mending their toys,
  And shares with His neighbours a countryman's joys;
But, out on the hill-tops, His Sonship He knows
  With God the immortal, who all things bestows.

The Village Carpenter

He was in the world, and the world was made by Him, and the world knew Him not.

St. John 1 : 10

8.7.8.7.

1 Hear the sound of plane and hammer
    In the workshop by the way!
  'Tis our Lord engaged in labour
    At the breaking of the day.

2 Village workmen bid good morning
    As they pass the open door,
  Knowing not that He shall judge them
    When the earth shall be no more.

3 Children enter at the noonday,
    Bringing toys for Him to mend;
  Little dreaming that the sunlight
    Was created by this Friend.

4 By Thy lowliness, Lord Jesus,
    Raise our life to heights sublime,
  Based upon eternal values,
    Even in this vale of time.

9

V

The Ministry of Jesus

Lorelei. 9.6.9.6.D.

1 Our Saviour came down the white highway
    When summer skies were blue,
And looked in the nooks and the crannies
    Where scarlet flowers grew :
And down by the shore, where the waters
    Were blue as heaven above,
Apostles He found, among fishers,
    And shared with them His love.

2 He took them for walks through the cornfields,
    And let them eat the corn
As David had eaten the shewbread
    When hungry and forlorn :
He pointed to lilies that toil not,
    Nor garments ever make,
For flowers, as God's little children,
    Are clothed for love's sweet sake.

3 The sparrows men sold in the market
    Were known to God, He said,
And He who gives clothing to lilies
    To birds gives daily bread :
And so with His band of disciples
    Through town and field Christ went,
Till men saw with awe and with wonder
    That God His Son had sent.

The Friend of Children

1 Along a sunlit Eastern road
  A crowd of children go,
And every heart is light with joy
  And every eye aglow;
For never such a day has been
  Since flowers began to grow.

2 They follow after Christ the Lord
  Who makes all sadness flee,
Who heals the sick, the deaf, the lame,
  And makes the blind to see;
With shout and song they follow Him
  Through ancient Galilee.

3 And down the ages He has come,
  And walks our land today,
And still the children follow Him
  As flowers follow May;
For every child finds life and joy
  On His enchanted way.

The Cornfield Way
St Matthew 12 : 1

1 O Son of God, who, on a Sabbath day,
With Thy disciples took the cornfield way.
And gave them of the golden food to eat;
For such a journey, Saviour, make us meet!

2 By loom and forge Thy presence we have felt,
And in the market place our thoughts have knelt
Before Thee at the gracious break of morn :
But, Lord, to walk with Thee 'mid ripening corn!

3 To see sweet Nature on a day of rest,
When she in cloth of gold is richly drest,
And share her bounty when Thou art her Guest!
With such felicity may we be blest?

4 To walk with Thee through fields or woodlands wild,
And listen to the wind as would a child,
Is to be born again, born from above,
And share with Thee the bread and wine of love.

By the Sea

D.C.M.

1   Where Galilee's blue waters lie,
      A voice so sweet is heard
  That children leave their merry games
      And listen to each word!
  The workmen plodding on their way
      Forget the passing hours,
  And stand entranced, while Jesus speaks
      Of God, and men, and flowers.

2   The world grows fairer as He speaks
      And God comes very near;
  The waves lie calm as if they heard;
      The birds lose all their fear;
  The face of Labour wears a smile;
      The sorrowful grow calm;
  The troubled mind finds welcome rest;
      The wounded heart finds balm.

3   O Jesus, in these later days,
      Let Thy sweet voice be heard;
  For Labour wears a troubled face,
      And faints with hope deferred;
  The aching heart no solace finds,
      The sinful soul no rest;
  O come in power, that earth may be
      With heaven's own radiance blest.

In the Market Place
St Matthew 20 : 1-16

L.M.

1 O Saviour, when we have no work,
 And cannot find it though we seek,
 And like a lamp that burneth low
 Our courage grows each day more weak :

2 When hope and strength are failing fast
 And every door we try is barred;
 Stand by us in the fading light,
 From doubt, despair and sin to guard.

3 In Salem's market-place Thy glance
 Fell kindly on the man unhired
 Who idle stood eleven hours;
 Not losing heart, though faint and tired.

4 With Thee the will counts as the deed,
 And labour sought is labour wrought :
 'They also serve who stand and wait'
 To labour, though the days bring nought.

VI

The Garden of Gethsemane
St Matthew 16 : 21-24

8.5.8.5.

1 Where the olive grove stood darkly
    Thou, O Christ, didst pray;
And upon Thine upturned features
    Fell the moon's soft ray.

2 Drops of blood were on Thy forehead,
    Brought by anguish sore;
Yet Thy burden Thou didst shoulder,
    Lord whom we adore.

3 When to follow Thee brings sorrow,
    Pain and social loss;
Let us watch Thee in the garden
    Taking up Thy Cross.

4 Though forsakings and betrayals
    Follow on Thy will,
May we tread the path of duty,
    Faithful to Thee still.

VII

Calvary

Jesus whom they slew and hanged on a tree
Acts 10 : 39

1   All nature shared the tragedy
When Jesus died upon a tree
That once, with leaf and blossom gay,
Shed fragrance o'er life's common way.

2   For common gain men took the life
Of this fair tree with none at strife;
And shorn of blossom, leaf and scent,
To its dark destiny it went.

3   A thing of life and beauty came
To be a Cross of vilest shame—
An instrument on which to hang
The Christ Whose birth the angels sang.

4   A tree that brought forth blossoms fair
Was made man's sin and shame to share :
A tree, from Bethlehem perchance,
That knew the children's song and dance.

5   But now with Christ is glorified
The broken tree on which He died—
A symbol sacred and supreme
To those who pray and those who dream.

The Night of Good Friday

*Now in the place where He was crucified there was a garden;
and in the garden a new sepulchre; there laid they Jesus for
the sepulchre was nigh at hand.*

St John 19 : 41-42

Stille Nacht. 76.77.7.

1　All is still : clouds, virgin white,
　　Veil the moon once so bright :
　　Night, with sorrow strangely still,
　　Drapes with shadows Calvary's hill;
　　　For, on a Cross, Jesus died.

2　Crucified !　Jesus no more
　　On the sea, or the shore,
　　Walks abroad to bless and save
　　Men from sin or whelming wave;
　　　For, in a garden, He lies.

3　Oh how still earth has become,
　　While He sleeps in His tomb !
　　Nightingales, as still as death,
　　Check their rich, melodious breath :
　　　For, in a garden, He sleeps.

4　Let Him sleep :　rest He has won :
　　All His work now is done :
　　Yet, three days, then we shall see
　　Him, again, in Galilee,
　　　For, from the grave, He will rise.

VIII

The Resurrection

10.10.10.10. Dactylic.

1   Wake from your slumbers ye men of good will;
    Night has departed from Calvary's hill;
    Jesus is risen; dispersed is the gloom;
    Bright is the garden, and radiant the tomb.

2   Darkness no longer the world holds in thrall;
    Day is now breaking, and breaking for all;
    Hills, which the armies of evil once trod,
    Now are aflame with the chariots of God.

3   Landward and seaward the world is alight;
    Wrong and oppression are now taking flight;
    Freedom and Justice and Truth unconfined
    Shall to all nations now speed like the wind.

4   Victory shall follow the banners of peace;
    War shall be banished and enmity cease;
    Men shall be brothers in workshop and field,
    Sharing together the products they yield.

5   Children, whom Jesus once throned on His knee,
    Shall from all forms of enslavement be free;
    Poor, backward races, no Power shall oppress,
    Blessings unbounded shall all men possess.

When the Daylight Wanes
St John 20 : 19

Sandon.   10.4.10.4.10.10.

1   O Risen Saviour, when the daylight wanes,
    Go Thou before,
To meet us in our streets and quiet lanes
    Or by the shore;
Among Thine own at eventide to be;
    As in the ancient days in Galilee.

2   'In England's green and pleasant land' Thy feet
    The saints have heard;
And, where our rocky shores the waters meet,
    Have caught Thy word;
In old cathedral towns and cities new,
    A Face is seen that Bethany once knew.

3   No more in Galilee we look for Thee,
    O Risen Lord;
In every land and on each moonlit sea
    Thy voice is heard;
And when Thy saints are gathered in Thy Name,
    Closer Thou art to each than fire to flame.

'The Lord is Risen Indeed'
St Luke 24 : 28-36

L.M.

1 We leave Thy house but leave not Thee,
   For Thou wilt ever with us be;
   For time nor space can us divide,
   Or take us from our Shepherd's side.

2 Thy flock we are : Thy house our fold
   Where we together Thee behold :
   Yet, when we scatter o'er life's fields,
   Thy presence sweet communion yields.

3 The Upper Room has not decayed,
   Each stone has now a million made :
   In every land disciples meet,
   And see Thy wounded hands and feet.

4 Though lamps go out, and home we turn,
   We feel our hearts within us burn;
   And, day far spent, the very street
   Rings, like Emmaus, with Thy feet.

Above the Hills of Time

Londonderry Air. 11.10.11.10.D.

1 Above the hills of time the Cross is gleaming,
    Fair as the sun when night has turned to day;
And from it love's pure light is richly streaming,
    To cleanse the heart and banish sin away.
To this dear Cross the eyes of men are turning
    Today as in the ages lost to sight;
And so for Thee, O Christ, men's hearts are yearning
    As shipwrecked seamen yearn for morning light.

2 The Cross, O Christ, Thy wondrous love revealing,
    Awakes our hearts as with the light of morn,
And pardon o'er our sinful spirits stealing
    Tells us that we, in Thee, have been reborn.
Like echoes to sweet temple bells replying,
    Our hearts, O Lord, make answer to Thy love;
And we will love Thee with a love undying,
    Till we are gathered to Thy home above.

The Light of the World

Dedicated to R. N. F. Evans (Religious Films Ltd.), with happy memories of our friendship as workers together in the pioneer days of religious films.

Slane 10.10.10 10. Dactylic.   *Traditional Irish Har. by L. L. Dix.*

1 Dawn, like a pilgrim in grey mantle clad,
   Lights with his lamp a world silent and sad :
   Nature awakes, and birds break into song
   Worshipping God to whom praises belong.

2 So, to mankind, lost in darkness and doubt,
   Comes the Lord Jesus and night puts to rout :
   Light of the World, He brings freedom and peace.
   Pardon for sin, and the joys that ne'er cease.

3 He is our Way and the Light of our day :
   He is our Life and our bread and our stay :
   Giving His body to death on the tree
   He hath redeemed us and set our souls free.

4 Word of the Father, He all things hath made :
   Sunlight and moonlight and stars that ne'er fade :
   Lilies and roses and trees in the dale !
   This is our Saviour whose love shall prevail.

5 Jesus, O Jesus, Thine own make my heart,
   Ever in service to be where Thou art :
   Bread to be broken Thy hungry to feed :
   Clay in Thy hands where the blind stand in need.

The Earth a Temple

And He said unto them, Go ye into all the world, and preach the Gospel to every creature. . . . And they went forth, and preached everywhere, the Lord working with them, and confirming the word with signs following.

St Mark 16 : 15 & 20

C.M.

1 All ye who know that on the Cross
    Christ did salvation bring,
Lift up your heart, lift up your voice,
    And make the whole world ring.

2 O make the whole world ring with joy,
    And spread the news around;
Till every man shall hear the song
    That we, in Christ, have found.

3 The song of our redemption raise,
    And storm high heaven's gate,
Till angels in amaze look out
    At Man's exalted state.

4 For we, the fallen, now may rise
    And stand with Christ on high,
In robes made white beneath His Cross,
    And hallelujah cry.

5 A thousand hallelujahs cry,
    O ye from sin set free;
And make the winds your story tell
    O'er every land and sea.

6 In songs that thrill and throb with joy,
    Your heart and voice upraise;
And make the earth a temple vast
    In which to sing His praise.

One, two, four or six hymns by Mr. Tiplady are in the church hymnals used at divine worship by more than fourteen million church members in America and Canada. Eleven *different* ones are used.

.   .   .   .   .

The Federal Council of the Churches of Christ in America represents 25 denominations and more than 27 million church members. In its supplementary hymnal: *Hymns of the Rural Spirit,* there are 97 authors and translators; 81 have one hymn each, 13 have two each, J. S. B. Monsell has three, Samuel Longfellow four and Thomas Tiplady five.

.   .   .   .   .

There are four hymns by Mr Tiplady in *The Girls' Life Brigade Hymnal;* four in *The Divine Healing Hymnal* sanctioned by the Archbishops of Armagh and Dublin; and seven in *Masterpieces of Religious Verse* (Harper Bros., New York and London).

.   .   .   .   .

The Light of the World is circulated as a film-strip by Religious Films Ltd. in England and, by arrangement with another film organization, in America. The hymn was recorded as sung at Westminster Central Hall by The Wiseman Choir under the leadership of Dr Brockless.